Tsunami

Monster Waves

Mary Dodson Wade

AMERICAN
DISASTERS

Enslow Publishers, Inc.

40 Industrial Road   PO Box 38
Box 398   Aldershot
Berkeley Heights, NJ 07922   Hants GU12 6BP
USA   UK
http://www.enslow.com

For Bruce and Liane, who brought me Hawaii

Library of Congress Cataloging-in-Publication Data

Wade, Mary Dodson.
   Tsunami : monster waves / Mary Dodson Wade.
      p. cm. — (American disasters)
   Includes bibliographical references and index.
   ISBN 0-7660-1786-9
   1. Tsunamis—Hawaii—History—20th century—Juvenile literature.
   [1. Tsunamis—Hawaii.] I.Title. II. Series.
   GC220.3 .W34   2001
   551.47'024'09969—dc21

                                        2001001816

Printed in the United States of America

10 9 8 7 6 5

To Our Readers:
We have done our best to make sure all Internet addresses in this book were active and appropriate when we went to press. However, the author and the publisher have no control over and assume no liability for the material available on those Internet sites or on other Web sites they may link to. Any comments or suggestions can be sent by e-mail to comments@enslow.com or to the address on the back cover.

"School Boy from up Mauka" © Juliet S. Kono. Reprinted with permission. Taken from *Tsunami Years* (Honolulu: Bamboo Ridge Press, 1995), pp. 68–69.

Illustration Credits: AP/Wide World Photos, pp. 45, 46, 47, 48, 50; © Corel Corporation, p. 1; DigialGlobe, pp. 42, 44; Harold L. Wade, pp. 29, 34, 35, 37; Hokusai, p. 23; Masami Takemoto, Consul-General of Japan at Houston, Texas, p. 11; Mrs. Harry A. Simms, Sr./ National Geophysical Data Centers (NGDC), pp. 6, 22; National Oceanic and Atmospheric Administration (NOAA)/ Department of Commerce, pp. 12, 38, 39; National Oceanic and Atmospheric Administration (NOAA)/EDIS, p. 27; U.S. Army Corps of Engineers/ National Geophysical Data Centers (NGDC), p. 8; U.S. Coast Guard/ National Geophysical Data Centers (NGDC), p. 17; U.S. Department of the Interior/ National Geophysical Data Centers (NGDC), p. 14; U.S. Geological Survey/ National Geophysical Data Centers (NGDC), p. 24; U.S. Navy/ National Geophysical Data Centers (NGDC), p. 20.

Cover Illustration: AP/Wide World Photos.

Contents

1 "A Monstrous Wall of Water" 7

2 Creating a Killer 10

3 No Place to Hide 19

4 Disaster on the Big Island 26

5 Learning from Tragedy 32

6 Disaster in the Indian Ocean 41

Other Tsunami Disasters 52

Chapter Notes 53

Glossary 58

Further Reading 60

Internet Addresses 61

How You Can Help 62

Index 63

Waves of devastation crash upon the beachfront near the Puumaile Tuberculosis Hospital on the island of Hawaii on April 1, 1946.

CHAPTER 1

"A Monstrous Wall of Water"

Water. That's what everyone there remembered about the morning of April 1, 1946. Dr. Francis Shepard recalled it well. The noted marine geologist was in Hawaii as part of a team studying the effects of atomic bomb tests on a remote Pacific island. He and his wife awakened to a hissing sound as loud as a dozen freight trains. They watched the water smash through the front of their cottage. A large wave carried their refrigerator, still upright, out the back door and set it down in a cane field.

As the Shepards fled their home, they were shocked to see that there was almost nothing left of the nearby house to the east. Just as they reached the safety of a road higher up, they watched helplessly as the water overwhelmed their cottage on Oahu's north shore. Then another wave like a "monstrous wall of water" swept toward them, "flattening the cane field with a terrifying sound."[1]

Sixteen-year-old Yasu Gusukuma was on the "Big

Island" of Hawaii. She saw houses swirling in a "boiling" sea.[2]

Kapua Heuer's house was on the Big Island too. It sat on a sea cliff thirty feet above the harbor in Hilo. That morning, her daughter called out, "Mommy, why is there no water in the ocean?" From the edge of their cliff, they could see the water disappearing. Then a "great black

*A*ll of the houses on the main street facing Hilo Bay on the island of Hawaii were swept across the street by the 1946 tsunami, crashing into the buildings on the opposite side.

wall" came back. With a roar, the water slammed into buildings, the lighthouse, and the railroad bridge. "Oh, that's good-bye to Hilo," Heuer said.[3]

Masao Uchima saw a fifteen-foot wave roll in. "I thought the whole island was sinking."[4] Behind it came a wall of water that stretched across the whole bay.

Paul Tallett noticed the strange dark-green color. He saw the water recede, tumbling like big boulders as it went. He fled home yelling, "A big sea is coming."[5] And it did—a mountainous moving wall of water that did not break but came directly on shore.

The "big sea" arrived without warning. It reached a height of fifty-five feet on the northeast coast of the Big Island. But other islands felt its force as well. Molokai had fifty-three foot waves. Waves on Kauai reached forty-five feet.[6]

The disaster happened on April 1, but it was no April Fool's joke. People lost their lives because the Hawaiian Islands are sitting ducks in the path of monster waves called tsunamis.

It was not the state's first tsunami, nor will it be the last. But it was Hawaii's worst one so far. Monster waves brought death and destruction that day.

CHAPTER 2

Creating a Killer

Hawaii is a magic place, with picture-perfect sunsets, palm trees, sandy beaches, and surfers hanging ten on forty-foot curling waves. Rainbows appear almost daily from an afternoon rain shower. Tropical flowers bloom everywhere. Houses need almost no heating or air-conditioning. Even the island names are musical: Oahu, Maui, Kauai, Molokai, Lanai, and the Big Island of Hawaii. It is practically heaven on earth.

Why, then, did 158 people lose their lives there on that April morning in 1946? What happened to cause millions of dollars in damage? Why were the people not warned?

The answer can be found in the ocean.

Hawaii lies in the middle of the Pacific Ocean. Its islands were formed by volcanoes, but volcanoes did not cause the deaths that day. Massive waves were the culprit. This series of gigantic waves, called tsunamis, are the most powerful waves in the world.[1]

The word *tsunami* is made up of two Japanese words. *Tsu* means "harbor," and *nami* means "wave."[2] Although the effects of a tsunami are seen most clearly in a harbor, that is not where tsunamis begin. They start in the ocean or in another body of water connected to the ocean.

Because tsunamis occur in the ocean, some people called them tidal waves. That is misleading, because tsunamis do not have anything to do with ocean tides. Tides are caused by the gravitational pull of the moon and the sun.

Most tsunamis are caused by water movement after an undersea earthquake.[3] That has led some scientists to call

*T*he two Japanese characters representing the word *tsunami*: The top, *tsu*, means "harbor", while the bottom, *nami*, means "wave".

them seismic sea waves. The word *seismic* refers to earthquakes, but that name is not exactly correct either. Other things besides undersea earthquakes can cause tsunamis.

For example, a volcanic eruption near the ocean can create a tsunami. The largest volcano-related tsunami happened when Krakatau (also called Krakatoa) in

Indonesia exploded in 1883. Seawater rushed into the crater left by the explosion. This created a blast of steam so violent that it was heard as far away as Australia. The force caused a tsunami with waves several hundred feet high. A total of 36,417 people died.[4]

On rare occasions, falling meteorites or huge rocks slides can push aside enough water to cause a tsunami. A rockslide in Lituya Bay, Alaska, in 1958 caused a wave that left debris nearly a third of a mile up the face of the mountain across the bay. This run-up, a high point that the water reaches, is the highest ever recorded for a tsunami.[5]

Sometimes underwater landslides are the source of a tsunami. Tons of rock shake loose and slide into deep

Tsunami damage in Kodiak, Alaska, following the Good Friday earthquake in 1964.

trenches on the sea floor. When this is coupled with an earthquake, the tsunami gets much larger.

Normally, an undersea earthquake must measure 7.8 or larger on the Richter Scale to cause a tsunami. In 1998 a medium-sized earthquake occurred off the coast of Papua New Guinea. Within five minutes, a thirty-five-foot wall of water came ashore. It killed more than two thousand people.

The amount of destruction surprised scientists. Then they found evidence of a landslide into a deep ocean trench nearby. The slide greatly increased the action of the water.[6]

Most tsunamis occur in the Pacific Ocean. Japan has been keeping records of them for two thousand years. However, they have also been known to occur in the Atlantic Ocean and the Mediterranean Sea. Tsunamis occur more often in the Pacific, however, because 80 percent of the world's earthquakes occur around the Pacific Rim.[7]

Earthquakes occur as a result of the earth's composition. The earth's surface is made up of solid land masses called tectonic plates. The plates ride on molten rock deep in the earth. When the plates move, the edges grind against each other. Sometimes the two plates get stuck. The slipping stops, but the force keeps building. Finally, the plates break loose with a jolt. This is when an earthquake occurs. Most of the time, the plates move sideways.[8] This type of movement will not cause a tsunami.

*F*urther example of the damage caused by the earthquake-generated tsunami that struck Alaska on Good Friday, March 27, 1964.

Sometimes, however, the edge of one plate rides up over the edge of another. This forces the second plate down. One part of the ocean floor lifts. All the water above it lifts upward. The other part of the ocean floor sinks, and the water just above it drops down as well.[9]

Imagine a pan full of water. If you could suddenly drain one side of the pan, the water on the other side would rush over to fill up the space. When this happens in the ocean, an incredible amount of water is moved. A tsunami is caused.

On April 1, 1946, there was a frightful displacement of water. An earthquake sent out an enormous wave that raced through the darkness. The first place it hit was Unimak Island in Alaska.

The Aleutian Islands swing out from the west coast of Alaska. They look like an outstretched arm. Unimak Island sits far out from the mainland. Ninety miles off the coast, a deep trench slices across the ocean floor.

The area near Unimak is a dangerous place for ships. The United States installed a lighthouse at a desolate place called Scotch Cap.

Just six years before the tsunami struck, the government had built a new lighthouse. The building was made of reinforced concrete. A powerful beacon in its five-story tower blinked every fifteen seconds. There was also a fog signal for passing ships. The lighthouse was forty feet above sea level. Five members of the Coast Guard lived there and tended the light. Another sixty feet up on the bluff above the lighthouse there was a radio direction-finding (DF) station. This was also maintained by a Coast Guard crew.

To combat boredom, the crews often played cards together. One of the DF crew had been at the lighthouse on the evening of March 31. A little after midnight, he left and walked up the hill to his sleeping quarters. It was just another night in this lonely place.

That totally changed less than two hours later. At 1:30 A.M., a tremor shook the area. Instruments all over the world, even in Hawaii, recorded the quake. The shaking lasted almost a minute. It was strong enough to knock things off shelves.

The operator at the DF station called down to the lighthouse. The crew below assured the operator that everything was okay, but nothing could have been further from the truth.

Twenty-seven minutes later, the earth heaved again. The edge of a tectonic plate had snapped off. It plunged down into the Aleutian trench. The sea floor dropped, and the tsunami began its journey of destruction.

Tsunamis move at incredible speed. They strike with unbelievable power. The waves fan out in much the same way water does when a rock is dropped into a pond. However, the area directly in front of the source of the wave will feel its main force.[10]

Oddly enough, the lifted water actually splits. One wave goes in one direction, and the other wave goes the opposite way.

A wave that travels long distances before it strikes land is called a distant tsunami. On April 1, 1946, Hawaii felt the force as a distant tsunami. A local tsunami strikes much more quickly. This is because it has a much shorter distance to travel. In the darkness of the Aleutian night that April 1, a local tsunami bore down on Unimak Island.

Twenty minutes was all it took. At 2:18 A.M., a wall of water rose out of the ocean.[11] A gigantic wave smashed into the Scotch Cap lighthouse. The wave rode up the face of the cliff and flooded the engine room of the DF station. The crew scrambled to higher ground.

From their high perch, the men strained to see the lighthouse beacon. No light shone in the darkness. No fog

The Scotch Cap Lighthouse on Unimak Island, Alaska, as it appeared before the 1946 tsunami (inset) and after. All five occupants were killed as the five-story lighthouse was almost completely erased from the face of the earth.

signal sounded. What had happened to their friends? The crew returned to the DF station and tried to contact the lighthouse. There was no response to telephone calls or to radio messages.

As soon as it was light enough, the men walked to the edge of the cliff. An unbelievable sight greeted them. The lighthouse was gone. The only thing left was part of the back wall of the building.

The DF station's radio operator sent out a message:

TIDAL WAVE PRECEDED BY EARTHQUAKE COMPLETELY DESTROYED SCOTCH CAP LIGHT STATION WITH LOSS OF ALL HANDS X TOP OF WAVE STRUCK THIS UNIT CAUSING EXTENSIVE DAMAGE BUT NO LOSS OF LIFE. . . . WILL SEARCH FOR BODIES OF SCOTCH CAP PERSONNEL AS SOON AS POSSIBLE X REQUEST INSTRUCTION.[12]

Scotch Cap lighthouse and its crew of five had been wiped off the face of the earth by a massive tsunami wave.

CHAPTER 3

No Place to Hide

While one massive wave swept away Scotch Cap lighthouse, an identical wave was speeding toward Hawaii on its own journey of destruction. This one raced through the darkness at 490 miles per hour. Tsunamis move extremely fast in deep water. In the open ocean, they may reach speeds of 800 kilometers (almost 500 miles) an hour.[1]

Tsunamis strike Hawaii from all directions. Twelve damaging tsunamis have slammed into the islands in the past one hundred years.[2] The ones that come from the northwest begin off the coasts of Russia and Japan. Those from Peru and Chile pound the islands from the southeast. But the worst ones come from Alaska to the north.

The killer tsunami that started in the Aleutian Islands on April 1, 1946, took the highest number of lives of all. And it came without warning.

Oddly enough, it is almost impossible to detect a

tsunami in the deep ocean. Tsunami waves in mid-ocean are usually no more than two to four feet high.[3] Ships pass over them without noticing anything unusual.

Even fishing boats are not disturbed. On that April morning, a Hawaiian fisherman was in his boat just off the coast. He felt nothing unusual as he moved along. As

Parking meters on this Hilo street were bent backward by the force of a tsunami generated by an earthquake off the coast of Chile on May 22, 1960.

he looked out to sea, everything seemed calm. Then he turned toward land and saw a huge wave crashing ashore.

From the air, however, the pilot of a small patrol plane saw something that looked like a line in the ocean. He radioed his base in Honolulu. Fellow servicemen laughed. April Fool!

However, the pilot was told to fly lower for a closer look. By the time he swooped down, the line had disappeared. The wave had outrun his plane.

Less than five hours after the wave left Alaska, it struck Kauai's north coast. The time was 5:55 A.M. Seventeen people died there.[4]

On the south side of the island, workers at the McBryde Sugar Company were sent by their supervisor to watch the tsunami. They too thought he was playing an April Fool joke.

From the cliff, they saw that the ocean had drained away. Fish were flopping in places where water had been. Then a huge wave came in. Water sped up the valley, snapping trees as it went.

When the water flowed out again, the men foolishly climbed down past fish tangled in tree branches. But they scrambled back when they saw the wave returning.

Climbing down was a very unwise thing to do. Many people have lost their lives by going down to the exposed seabed after a tsunami has passed by. The water returns too fast for them to escape.

Trying to outrun a wave is only one mistake people make. Some people have lost their lives because they

A monstrous wave of water strikes Hawaii less than five hours after leaving Alaska on April 1, 1946.

thought there was only one wave to a tsunami. A tsunami is a series of waves, maybe as many as ten.[5]

Even those people who know that more waves are coming may think they are safe. After all, the first wave did not reach them. But the waves vary in size. Often the third to eighth waves are the largest.[6] People who escaped the first wave can be overwhelmed by later ones.

Sometimes people get into trouble because they think that a tsunami is over. As time goes by, they feel safe returning to their homes and businesses. The time between waves varies. Some may be five minutes apart, or the time between one wave and the next may be as much as an hour and a half.[7]

Arrival times for waves depend on the distance between crests. A wave crest is the top of the wave.

Tsunami crests are much farther apart than the crests of waves caused by wind. Wind waves are rarely more than a thousand feet apart. That is about the length of two city blocks. A tsunami can have wave lengths of 60 to 120 miles.[8]

There is a popular notion that tsunamis are always giant curling waves. That is the form many people remember from a famous eighteenth-century painting by a Japanese artist named Hokusai. His painting shows a giant spilling wave towering over Mount Fuji. This painting is really one of a series of paintings that the artist did of this famous mountain in Japan. It is really the painting of a wind wave. But the painting has come to represent the way most people think of tsunami waves.

Japanese artist Hokusai's famous painting, *The Great Wave off Kanagawa on the Tokkaido*, from *The Thirty-six Views of Fuji*. This painting has come to represent how most people perceive tsunamis.

*T*sunamis generate a tremendous amount of force. The 1964 tsunami that struck Prince William Sound, Alaska was so powerful it drove a plank through a truck tire, as pictured above.

Actually, a tsunami may arrive at any part of the wave motion. Sometimes the trough of the wave arrives first. The trough is the low space in front of the crest. When the trough comes in first, the water drains away from the land. Sea creatures are stranded. Many people who have witnessed a tsunami mention fish flopping.

But the most common way that a tsunami arrives is as a flood of water. It just keeps coming farther and farther inland.

Sometimes the wave comes in as a bore. The bore is a tumbling wall of water with a churning top. The bore is created when the crest and the trough come in together. Regardless of what form it takes, the water has tremendous force. It crushes whatever is in front of it.

The force comes from the way the tsunami affects the water. Wind waves, even in large storms, disturb the water to a depth of no more than five hundred feet.[9] A tsunami moves water all the way from the ocean floor to the surface. As it speeds across the ocean, the wave loses little of its power.

When the wave reaches land, however, it slows down. Millions of tons of water are moving. The slowing wave still has all the force behind it. Since the force can't move forward, the water piles up higher. Waves become huge. By the time they get to shore, they are enormous and deadly.

Slowing down also moves the crests closer together. Incoming waves may resemble a giant staircase.[10]

On that April day in 1946, the tsunami slowed as it struck Kauai. But it still had enough strength to send four-teen people to their deaths on Maui. By 6:30 A.M., it had claimed six more victims on Oahu.[11]

Then the wave headed for the Big Island. It was as if the tsunami had saved its deadliest fury for the last island in the chain.

CHAPTER 4

Disaster on the Big Island

Shortly before 7:00 A.M., the tsunami struck the largest of the islands. Before the morning was over, more than a hundred people would die there.[1]

Hilo, on the eastern shore, suffered the most. Its funnel-shaped harbor brought in the tsunami with incredible force. Businesses on Kamehameha Avenue, the main street of Hilo, were smashed. The train station disappeared. Railroad cars were thrown into the harbor. Wharf warehouses splintered. Docks collapsed.

The U.S.S. *Brigham Victory* sat in Hilo harbor carrying fifty tons of dynamite. The first wave broke the mooring lines that held the ship to the dock. The crew started the engines to try to get out of the port. When Steward Wayne Rasmussen saw the first wave come in, he grabbed his camera. One of his photographs shows a helpless dock worker facing the wave that would engulf him.[2]

The *Brigham Victory* steered around reefs to get into the ocean. On the way out of the harbor, the ship's crew

Wayne Rasmussen's famous photo of the 1946 tsunami bursting over Pier No. 1 in Hilo Harbor, Hawaii. The man indicated by the arrow was one of 158 fatalities.

rescued a truck driver who was unloading sugar. His truck was swept into the bay.

Tuk Wah Lee fled to the rafters of the warehouse when he saw the brown wall of water approaching. The wave ripped away the front of the building and shoved a barge through the back wall.

When the water receded, Lee climbed down. After missing a line thrown by the ship's crew, he jumped in to swim to the ship. Debris was all around. A wave lifted him enough so that he could scramble on deck before it flattened the building where he had been.[3]

Albert Yasuhara parked his soft-drink truck where he thought he would be safe. He was curious because he had heard that there were always three waves in a tsunami. After the second wave smashed buildings, Yasuhara saw that the bay was empty. He saw the third wave reach halfway up the coconut trees. He and others fled up the street, just ahead of the water.[4]

Jim Herkes stopped his car on the highway bridge over the Wailuku River. He and his brother watched a bore come up the small river. It struck the nearby railroad bridge and broke off one of the spans. When the wave retreated, the span sailed out under their feet. The next wave brought it back up the river. The railroad span came to rest 750 feet upstream.[5]

Bob "Steamy" Chow was a policeman on duty that morning. He saw the railroad span washing under the highway bridge. His job was to keep people out of the danger area. As he drove near the waterfront, water swirled underneath his car. He had the helpless feeling that he was being washed away, but he lived to tell about it.[6]

The tsunami damaged or destroyed thousands of homes. Ninety-six people were killed in Hilo. Hardest hit was the low-lying Japanese community, and the bayfront business district looked like a war zone.

At Anaehoomalu the waves took one more victim.

The total damage to the state of Hawaii amounted to $26 million in 1946 currency.[7] But no amount of money could pay for the damage done at Laupahoehoe.

This place, about thirty miles north of Hilo, takes its name from the lava rocks (pahoehoe) that formed the land. On that terrible day, the tsunami swept over the pahoehoe. It claimed four people in the village below the cliff. Fifteen schoolchildren and five teachers lost their lives as well.

The school sat on a peninsula jutting into the water. A seawall formed a level area for the baseball field. Teachers lived in cottages near the water.

The school day had not yet started. Some children were out on the playground. Others were standing on the seawall looking at a curious sight. The water had disappeared. The ocean floor was filled with all kinds of creatures.

*B*ob "Steamy" Chow and author Mary Dodson Wade stand outside the Pacific Tsunami Museum in March 2001.

Teacher Frank Kanzaki was eating breakfast at a friend's cottage. He saw a giant wave rise out of the ocean. He grabbed the friend's two little girls sitting at the table. The wave splintered the cottage. The water pulled one of the children out of his grasp. He never saw her again.[8]

Third grader Carol Billena was waiting in her classroom. She thought the boy who ran past her was yelling "tiger wave." She asked her older sister if she could go out and see it.

Her sister realized that he was saying "tidal wave." She pushed Carol out the door and pushed her up the hill. "Run, run, run!" she called. Carol looked back. Cottages were breaking apart in the "boiling" sea. She could see heads bobbing in the water.[9]

Martha Silva and her friend Janet De Caires went over to see turtles and fish washed up near the boys' bathroom. Janet wanted to go down to the water. "Stay with me," begged Martha. But Janet ran to catch up with her brother and sister. She got to the middle of the ballfield before water as high as the coconut trees poured in from all directions. Martha fled up the hill. The next time she saw Janet was in a makeshift morgue.[10]

Bunji Fujimoto thought it was an April Fool joke when students said that the ocean had disappeared. His little brother went down to look, but Bunji hung back. He saw the wall of water rise over the seawall. Bunji's little brother was never found.[11]

Poet Juliet Kono wrote a poem to honor the children who died at Laupahoehoe. Into it, she wove the children's story called *The Five Chinese Brothers.*

In the story each brother saves another brother's life because he can do special things. One can stretch his legs. Another can swallow the sea. It is only a story. Nobody was there to save the children at Laupahoehoe from the churning flood of water.

School Boy from up Mauka
by Juliet S. Kono

You ran outdoors
to look at the receding sea.
Open and bare,
it was as if the tale
of the Five Chinese Brothers
had come true, the story
your teacher had read to you.
Somewhere,
on the other side of the ocean,
the First Chinese brother
had drunk all the water.
And here, on this peninsula,
how everything glittered:
red stars, black sea urchins, pink anemones.
With pants rolled high,
shirt tucked in at the waist,
you walked into shallow water
and picked up the red, gold and silver fish;
papio, weke, aweoweo.
Fish for a good boy to take home.
Fish for supper.
"Look, look," you yelled to everyone,
pointing at your prizes.
A sudden roar.
As in the story,
the first Chinese brother
who could no longer hold the water,
let it rush out
and into our side of the world.
If I could, I'd have stretched my legs into stilts
like the third Chinese brother
and plucked you from the sea.
You dropped the colors from your hands.
You moved up to face the wave.
And in your wonder, all you could do
was gape and point at
what curled,
magnificently, above you

CHAPTER 5

Learning from Tragedy

Two hours after the tsunami hit Hawaii, the sea was calm again. By 9:00 A.M., boats were out picking up survivors. The grim task of identifying victims began. Only 115 bodies were ever found.[1]

Laupahoehoe tenth grader Herbert Nishimoto was lucky. He was pulled out of the ocean the next day. Herbert was a strong swimmer who loved to dive into the rough water near his home at Laupahoehoe. Three-foot waves were nothing to him. He knew when to breathe during a dive. But this wave was different. It sucked him into the ocean.

Herbert kicked off his jeans in order to swim better, but one pants leg got caught on a reef. Dazed by the battering, he recovered enough to know that sharks and debris were all around.

A bottle of cooking oil floated by. He had heard that swimmers greased their bodies, so he oiled himself.

Then, when part of a floor came by, he heaved himself onto it.

About 1:00 P.M., a seaplane dropped a raft down to him and two other students. The three climbed in, but they had no paddle. After drifting all night, the exhausted boys were pulled ashore by two strong swimmers.[2]

For many years it was thought that 159 people died in Hawaii because of the 1946 tsunami. Recently, researchers discovered that one child at Laupahoehoe had been counted twice. A young girl had been adopted by a Portuguese family, and her name had been changed. She had been listed by both her adopted family's name and her Japanese name.[3]

The survivors of the disaster did not want others to forget the fury of the waves. Some of them organized the Pacific Tsunami Museum, where they serve as volunteers. The museum is in the old First Hawaiian Bank building on Kamehameha Avenue. It stands in the area where the waves came ashore. Displays, photos, videos, and eyewitness accounts help visitors understand what happened. Policeman Bob "Steamy" Chow's knowledge of the town provided accuracy for the model of Hilo prior to the 1946 tsunami.[4] Each April, Tsunami Awareness Month, the museum sponsors a student essay contest.

The city of Hilo built a park at the waterfront rather than replace buildings there. This proved to be a wise move. The park was enlarged after the 1960 tsunami crushed more buildings.

The old Laupahoehoe school yard is a park too.

*T*he Pacific Tsunami Museum on Kamehameha Avenue in Hilo, Hawaii.

Students attend school in another area, but no one forgets what happened out on that peninsula. Waves crash on lava boulders near a monument honoring the students and teachers who died that day.

The tragedy brought worldwide reaction. People needed to know why these killer waves occur. The 1946 Hawaiian tsunami became the most studied tsunami in history.[5] But each one is different. Also, because they are rare, it has taken time to learn how they form and how they move.

The United States set up the Pacific Tsunami Warning Center (PTWC) in 1948. The center is located on Oahu at Eva Beach not far from Pearl Harbor. As part of the

National Oceanic and Atmospheric Administration (NOAA), it constantly records information about earthquakes and ocean water movement.

After 1960, when a Pacific-wide tsunami began in Chile, other nations formed the International Tsunami Warning System. This agency is under the direction of the United Nations. It is based in Honolulu and cooperates with PTWC. It publishes information to educate people about tsunamis.

*T*his monument now stands where the Laupahoehoe school yard once stood, in honor of those teachers and students who lost their lives in the 1946 tsunami.

PTWC is responsible for issuing alerts and warnings. Banks of satellite dishes bring information to its computers. E-mail, fax machines, and dedicated phone lines keep the staff in touch with other scientists all over the world.

Someone is on duty at all times. Staffers wear two pagers just in case one fails. They live in housing on the grounds so that they can respond quickly to an alarm.[6]

PTWC computers monitor information from nine hundred seismic stations around the world. Within minutes of an earthquake, everyone knows the location of the epicenter. PTWC checks data from a hundred tide stations outside Hawaii for signs of unusual surface water movement.[7]

For tsunamis, however, it is critical to know about water movement on the ocean floor. NOAA developed Deep-Ocean Assessment and Reporting of Tsunamis (DART) to check for movement in deep water. Five DARTs sit in the water off the coast of Alaska and the northwestern United States. Instruments lying fifteen thousand feet deep send signals to the surface. From there, the signal is relayed by satellite to PTWC every hour. However, when a tsunami wave passes by, DART reports immediately. Most tsunamis are too small to do any damage.[8]

If, however, a large earthquake occurs, PTWC watches carefully for deep water movement. If a large tsunami is detected, PTWC issues a watch for all areas in its path. A watch means that there is a possibility of a tsunami. People are advised by radio and television to listen for further announcements.

*T*he exterior of the Pacific Tsunami Warning Center
(PTWC) building at Eva Beach on Oahu.

Surface buoys like the one above are used by the National Oceanic and Atmospheric Administration (NOAA) for deep-water tsunami detection.

Hawaii is so far from other land areas that it usually has time to prepare. Scientists have learned that for every minute that a seismic (earthquake) wave takes to reach Hawaii, a tsunami will take one hour to arrive. In 1947, they developed a formal tsunami travel time chart.[9]

When a tsunami is confirmed, a warning plan goes into effect. Three hours before the tsunami is expected, Hawaiian Civil Defense sounds a three-minute steady siren. The siren sounds at hourly intervals and again a half hour before the wave is to arrive. People listen for announcements that update information.

This system works well for predicting distant tsunamis. However, local tsunamis, such as the one that wiped out Scotch Cap lighthouse, occur within minutes. For that reason, the West Coast and Alaska Tsunami Warning System alerts the northwest area of North America.

Until recently, it was assumed that the mainland United States was safe from a tsunami. Actually, the 1946 tsunami brushed the California coast and killed one man. Then, in 1960, the Chilean tsunami sent waves all the way to Mendocino, California.

Scientists are also concerned about tectonic plates that grind together off the coast of Washington and Oregon. The situation is ripe for a tsunami-producing earthquake.

In the 1980s, scientists found evidence that tsunamis

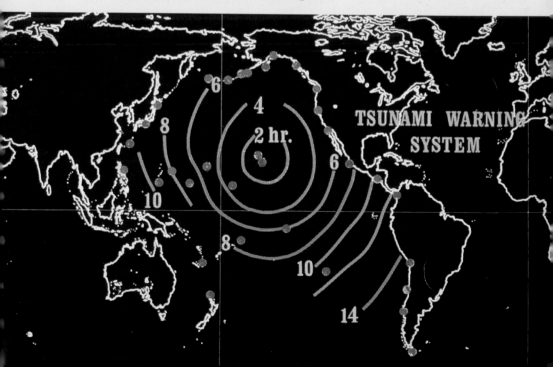

*A*n illustration of a tsunami time chart showing the distance (in hours) from various epicenters to Hawaii. An epicenter is a point on the earth's surface directly above the center of an earthquake.

had occurred in the region. An eleven-hundred-year-old layer of sand sits in Puget Sound in Washington State. Its arrangement matches the way that tsunami waves throw sand ashore.[10]

The Makah are a people who lived in Washington long before it became a state. They have a legend about the sea draining away. When the water returned, it covered everything except the mountaintops. People who were carried away by the waves set up a new village off the coast of Vancouver Island in present-day British Columbia, Canada. The Makah legend is supported by the fact that people in the two places have similar names. Also, Japanese records report a tsunami three hundred years ago and the area has telltale sand deposits of that age.[11]

Nothing can prevent a tsunami, but being informed can help people survive. The rules are simple: Seek high ground if there is a violent earthquake or if ocean water quickly drains away from land. Consult phone books for safe routes to evacuate low areas. Follow road signs to safety in coastal areas. Move ships and small boats to water six hundred feet deep or more.

Hawaii has learned hard lessons from the tsunamis it has experienced. More tsunamis will undoubtedly occur. But with a warning system in place, Hawaii should never have another tragedy like the one that happened on April 1, 1946.

CHAPTER 6

Disaster in the Indian Ocean

A few minutes after 3:00 P.M. on Christmas Day 2004, the instruments at PTWC indicated that a very large earthquake had occurred in the Indian Ocean. Across the International Date Line, at precisely 7:59 A.M. on December 26, 2004, a 750-mile long portion of the Burma tectonic plate had snapped off from the force of the Indian plate pushing against it. Usually moving only two and a half inches a year, the plates suddenly slipped fifty feet. The jolt caused by the movement resulted in a tsunami that caused loss of life as far as 3,000 miles away.[1]

The earthquake epicenter was just off the northwest coast of the Indonesian island of Sumatra. Unfortunately, the Indian Ocean has no equivalent of PTWC. There was no warning for the death and destruction radiating out from the earthquake.[2]

Staff at PTWC alerted other observatories in the Pacific about the earthquake but underestimated its size. The magnitude was later fixed at 9.3 on the Richter scale.

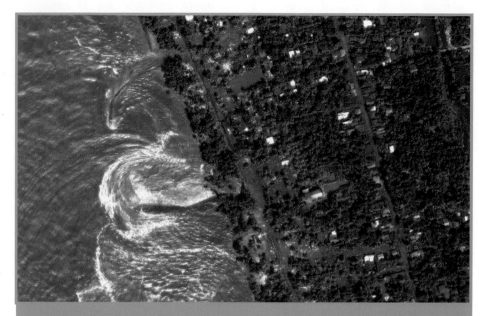

*A*n aerial view of the receding tsunami waters in Kalutara, Sri Lanka, on December 26, 2004. The tsunami was triggered by a magnitude 9 earthquake in the Indian Ocean—the fourth-largest quake in the last century.

Ten minutes after the event, run-up waves as high as 34.9 meters (113.4 feet) washed over the northwest coast of Sumatra.[3]

A fisherman from a small village on the Sumatran coast felt the quake shake his boat. He saw water receding from the shore in classic tsunami style. Then with thundering noise, swirling water slung his boat toward land. He was later found clinging to a coconut tree two miles away from where his boat had been.[4]

Tens of thousands of people were not so fortunate. Disaster fanned out to the rim of the Indian Ocean. It crossed to Africa and spread eastward to Thailand. At Banda Aceh on the northern tip of Sumatra, a nine-foot wall of water swept inland for six miles, burying the thriving town in mud. Coastal fishing villages disappeared. Two hours later Sri Lanka was hit. Within three and a half hours the whole of the Maldives had been washed over. Eight hours later, three hundred people died on the east coast of Africa. Waves traveling in the other direction struck the coast of Thailand where many Europeans had come for the holidays. Videos and photos taken by vacationers caught images of tsunami waves crashing into resort areas.[5]

In the aftermath, people searched frantically for missing relatives. Bodies were brought to temples and preserved with dry ice. Families poured over photographs of the dead posted on walls. Mass graves were dug. In Sri Lanka, nine grieving mothers claimed a tiny baby boy who had been found on a beach among the bodies and debris. The baby boy was called "Baby 81" because he was the 81st admission to Kalmunai Hospital on the day he was found. A judge ordered DNA tests to determine the real parents.[6]

Estimates of the dead and missing from all the effected countries on the rim of this disaster continued to rise. Six weeks after the event, the number had reached 280,000. Among them were at least 33 American known dead or presumed dead, and approximately 18 missing. The exact numbers of casualties will never be known. Some of Indonesia's thousands of islands are remote.

*A*t top is a satellite image of Banda Aceh before the tsunami hit. The image on the bottom shows what is left of Banda Aceh on December 28, 2004. Images courtesy DigitalGlobe.

There is no one left to tell what happened. Remarkably, twenty-five days after the quake, the sole survivor of one island was rescued. He had lived on coconuts.[7]

The remoteness of some islands made it difficult to assess damage. Nicobar and Andaman islands north of Sumatra were hit hard. Both islands are governed by India. There is little contact with outsiders in order to preserve the hunter-gatherer tribes living there. When Indian pilots flew over Andaman to look for survivors, inhabitants fired arrows at the helicopter.

Sailors aboard a U.S. Navy vessel prepare jugs of purified water for delivery to those in need in the city of Aceh, Sumatra, Indonesia, on January 4, 2005.

From all appearances, these people escaped real harm. Scientists believe that the traditions of these people, whose ancestors came out of Africa 30,000 to 60,000 years ago, taught them to seek higher ground when earthquakes occur. Wild animals seem to have survived by a similar instinct.[8]

A man collects fish that were washed up onto the streets of Vishakapatnam, India, by the tsunami on December 26, 2004.

As pictures and reports streamed in, the world responded with money, equipment, and medical supplies. Health organizations feared that epidemics of cholera and typhoid would occur from lack of clean water. American aircraft carrier *Lexington*, with capability for making fresh water, steamed to Sumatra and stayed until adequate water was available. Officials were grateful that no

*T*his man sits in the remains of his home on the island of Hafun on January 11, 2005. Almost all of the island's 4,500 inhabitants were left homeless by the tsunami.

widespread illness occurred. This may been because people did not crowd into refugee camps.[9]

In addition to health care, there was a need to rebuild roads, communication networks, businesses, houses, schools, and hospitals. Japan promised $500 million in aid. The United States set government aid at $350 million. In addition, President George W. Bush called on the American people to give. He appointed former presidents George H.W. Bush and Bill Clinton to head the Bush-

A tsunami victim surveys the collapsed homes in the coastal city of Pittawella in southern Sri Lanka on January 8, 2005.

Clinton Fund to encourage private donations through reputable charities. Celebrities also raised money at benefit concerts.[10]

But some things only time will heal. It will take years for rain to leach salt from flooded rice fields so that crops will grow again. Fish and shrimp farms will have to be rebuilt and stocked. Small farmers need livestock replaced. To coordinate this rebuilding, the Secretary-General of the United Nations appointed President Clinton as special tsunami envoy to accomplish the United Nation's goals.[11]

Even amidst all the devastation, however, there were moments of hope. On February 8, Baby 81 was taken to a clinic for DNA testing. The test was paid for by UNICEF (United Nations International Children's Emergency Fund). These tests would confirm that the child was four-month-old Abilass Jeyarajah, son of Murugupillai and Jenita Jeyarajah. (The baby's name was taken from the Sanskrit word *abhilasha*, which means "desire" or "aspiration.")[12]

Finally, on February 16, after seven agonizing weeks, a judge officially ruled that the boy was the Jeyarajahs' child. After the court hearing, the Jeyarajahs took Abilass to a Hindu temple, where they gave thanks for his safe return. They also stopped to visit the remains of their former home, where the raging tsunami waters tore Abilass from his mother Jenita's arms on December 26.

"Look how happy he is!" Murugupillai later

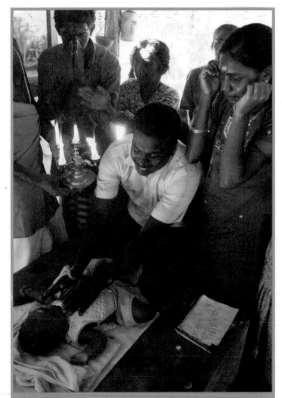

Murugupillai and Jenita Jeyarajah stand above their four-month-old son, Abilass, at a Hindu temple in Kalmunai, Sri Lanka, along with friends and family members on February 16, 2005.

proclaimed of his son. "After returning to us, he still hasn't cried."[13]

According to the estimates of the United Nations, about 12,000 of the 31,000 lives lost to the tsunami in Sri Lanka were children (an amazing 40 percent). Approximately 1,000 children were left orphaned and more than 3,000 others lost one parent.[14]

Scientists are still sorting out the effects that the great quake and tsunami had on our planet. For one, several islands were left slightly moved, including the island of Sumatra, which shifted "a little over a meter, perhaps a couple of meters."[15] This may not sound like much until one considers how much force is needed to move a land mass of Sumatra's size (1,060 miles long and 250 miles wide).

In addition, British naval ships collecting data off the coast of Sumatra discovered ruptures left in the seabed of the Indian Ocean several miles long. "These are features . . . like the Grand Canyon," observed scientist Tim Henstock. "You can see huge piles of mud maybe a few hundred meters thick."[16]

The quake also wobbled the earth on its axis, altering the rotation of the planet so that the length of the day was actually shortened. It was only reduced by 2.68 millionths of a second, however, so is not noticeable.[17]

The tragic loss of life and property caused by the tsunami led President George W. Bush to call for deep ocean warning buoys to be placed along America's coasts. It has also motivated countries along the Pacific Ring of Fire to develop a warning system that will alert them to future Indian Ocean tsunamis. Each country will have a warning system. The United Nations is encouraging a unified system for processing information. As Dr. Charles McCreery, director of PTWC, pointed out: "It's data coming from neighboring countries that's going to save you."[18]

Powerful forces of nature such as earthquakes and resulting tsunamis cannot be controlled. They cannot even be predicted with accuracy. But with tsunami education and adequate warnings in place, huge losses of life can be averted-lessons learned from Lapahoehoe and Banda Aceh.

Other Tsunami Disasters

DATE	PLACE	DISASTER
November 1, 1755	Lisbon, Portugal	Lisbon is almost completely destroyed as a result of a great earthquake and subsequent tsunami.
August 26, 1883	Indonesia	The eruption of the volcano Krakatau (Krakatoa) generates tsunami waves up to 120 feet high. These waves destroy almost 300 towns and villages, and drown more than 36,000 people.
November 18, 1929	Newfoundland, Canada	An undersea earthquake causes a tsunami that results in twenty-seven deaths and the equivalent of approximately $4 million in damages.
November 4, 1952	Kamchatka Peninsula, Russia	An earthquake off the coast of the Kamchatka Peninsula triggers a Pacific-wide tsunami. Damages in Hawaii are equivalent to more than $6 million.
March 9, 1957	Aleutian Islands, Alaska	An earthquake south of the Aleutian Islands of Alaska causes a Pacific-wide tsunami. Although no lives are lost, the Hawaiian islands suffer the equivalent of almost $30 million in damages.
May 22, 1960	Chile, South America	An earthquake off the coast of South Central Chile creates a Pacific-wide tsunami. The number of deaths attributed to the earthquake and tsunami are estimated between 490 and 2,290. Damage costs are estimated to be over half a billion dollars.
November 29, 1975	Hawaii	An earthquake off the Hawaiian coast triggers a tsunami. Nineteen campers are injured, and two die at Halape.
December 12, 1979	Colombia	An earthquake off the Pacific coast of Colombia and a subsequent tsunami destroy at least six fishing villages and cause hundreds of deaths.
July 17, 1998	Papua New Guinea	More than 3,000 die as a result of an earthquake-caused tsunami on the northern coast of Papua, New Guinea.

Chapter Notes

Chapter 1. "A Monstrous Wall of Water"

1. Francis P. Shepard, *The Earth Beneath the Sea* (Baltimore, Md.: Johns Hopkins University Press, 1959), p. 16.

2. Walter C. Dudley and Min Lee, *Tsunami!* 2d ed. (Honolulu: University of Hawaii Press, 1998), p. 10.

3. Kapua Wall Heuer, "Oral History Interview, September 4, 1998," *Tsunamis Remembered; Oral Histories of Survivors and Observers in Hawaii* (Honolulu: University of Hawaii at Manoa, 2000), vol. 1, pp. 651–652.

4. Masao Uchima, Video Tape 1, video transcript, Pacific Tsunami Museum.

5. Dudley and Lee, p. 32.

6. Karl V. Steinbrugge, *Earthquakes, Volcanoes, and Tsunamis: An Anatomy of Hazards* (New York: Kaskandia America Group, 1982), p. 246.

Chapter 2. Creating a Killer

1. Frank I. González, "Tsunami!" *Scientific American*, May 1999, p. 58.

2. "What does 'tsunami' mean?" *The Physics of Tsunamis*, n.d., <www.ngdc.noaa.gov/seg/hazard/tsu.shtml> (August 30, 2000).

3. González, p. 58.

4. George Pararas-Carayannis, "The Great Tsunami of August 26, 1883 from the Explosion of the Krakatau Volcano ('Krakatoa') in Indonesia," n.d., <http://www.geocities.com/CapeCanaveral/Lab/1029/Tsunami1883Krakatoa.html> (April 3, 2001).

5. Anne M. Rosenthal, "The Next Wave," *California Wild*, spring 1999, <http://www.calacademy.org/calwild/archives/spring99/tsunamis.htm> (August 30, 2000).

6. R. Monastersky, "Seabed Slide Blamed for Deadly Tsunami," n.d., <http://www.sciencenews.org/sn_arc99/8_14_99/fob2.htm> (August 30, 2000).

7. Karl V. Steinbrugge, *Earthquakes, Volcanoes, and Tsunamis: An Anatomy of Hazards* (New York: Kaskandia America Group, 1982), p. 235.

8. Walter C. Dudley and Min Lee, *Tsunami!* 2d ed. (Honolulu: University of Hawaii Press, 1998), p. 104.

9. "Life of a Tsunami," n.d., <http://walrus.wr.usgs.gov/tsunami/basics.html> (August 30, 2000).

10. Dudley and Lee, p. 321.

11. *Scotch Cap Lightstation Tsunami Disaster April 1, 1946*, n.d., <http://www.teleport.com/~alany/uscg/ltsta.html> (April 3, 2001).

12. Ibid.

Chapter 3. No Place to Hide

1. *Tsunami*, n.d., <http://library.thinkquest.org/16132/html/tsunami.html> (April 3, 2001).

2. Frank I. González, "Tsunami!" *Scientific American*, May 1999, p. 59.

3. Ibid.

4. Walter C. Dudley and Min Lee, *Tsunami!* 2d ed. (Honolulu: University of Hawaii Press, 1998), pp. 4, 41.

5. Anne M. Rosenthal, "The Next Wave," *California Wild*, spring 1999, <http://www.calacademy.org/calwild/archives/spring99/tsunamis.htm> (August 30, 2000).

6. Dudley and Lee, p. 118.

7. Ibid., p. 91.

8. *Tsunami*.

9. Dudley and Lee, p. 90.

10. Rosenthal.

11. Dudley and Lee, pp. 4, 41–42.

Chapter 4. Disaster on the Big Island

1. Walter C. Dudley and Min Lee, *Tsunami!* 2d ed. (Honolulu: University of Hawaii Press, 1998), p. 42.

2. Ibid., p. 14.

3. Ibid., p. 15.

4. Ibid., pp. 19–20.

5. Ibid., pp. 17, 43.

6. Robert "Steamy" Chow, interview with author, Pacific Tsunami Museum, Hilo, Hawaii, March 6, 2001.

7. Frank I. González, "Tsunami!" *Scientific American*, May 1999, p. 64.

8. Dudley and Lee, p. 8.

9. Ibid., p. 10.

10. Ibid., p. 11.

11. Ibid., p. 42.

Chapter 5. Learning from Tragedy

1. Walt Dudley and Scott C. S. Stone, *The Tsunami of 1946 and 1960 and the Devastation of Hilo Town* (Hilo: The Pacific Tsunami Museum, 2000), p. 16.

2. Herbert Nishimoto, video transcript, Pacific Tsunami Museum.

3. Donna Saiki, director, Pacific Tsunami Museum, e-mail to author, January 2, 2001.

4. Robert "Steamy" Chow, interview with author, Pacific Tsunami Museum, Hilo, Hawaii, March 6, 2001.

5. Walter C. Dudley and Min Lee, *Tsunami!* 2d ed. (Honolulu: University of Hawaii Press, 1998), p. 105.

6. Dr. Charles S. McCreery, interview with author, Pacific Tsunami Warning Center, Honolulu, Hawaii, March 5, 2001.

7. Dudley and Lee, p. 320.

8. Frank I. González, "Tsunami!" *Scientific American*, May 1999, pp. 322–325.

9. Dudley and Lee, p. 102.

10. "Cascadia Earthquakes and Tsunami Hazard Studies," n.d., <http://walrus.wr.usgs.gov/cascadia> (August 30, 2000).

11. "Native American Legends of Tsunamis in the Pacific Northwest," n.d., <http://walrus.wr.usgs.gov/tsunami/NAlegends.html> (August 30, 2000).

Chapter 6. Disaster in the Indian Ocean

1. "NOAA and the Indian Ocean Tsunami," n.d., <http://www.noaanews.noaa.gov/stories2004/S2358.htm> (February 3, 2005).

2. Ibid.; Michael Elliott, "Sea of Sorrow," *Time*, January 10, 2005, pp. 32–33.

3. "NOAA and the Indian Ocean Tsunami"; Dr. Charles McCreery, telephone interview with author, February 4, 2005; "The Distribution of the Tsunami Hights [sic] in Banda Aceh Measured by the Team Dr. Tsuji Leads," n.d., <http://www.eri.u-tokyo.ac.jp/namegaya/sumatera/surveylog/eindex.htm> (February 4, 2005).

4. *Time*, pp. 30–31.

5. Ibid., pp. 32–33.

6. Ibid., pp. 22–30; "Baby 81: Sri Lanka court orders DNA test," *India Times*, February 2, 2005, <http://timesofindia.indiatimes.com/articleshow/msid-1009629,curpg-2.cms> (February 4, 2005)

7. *ABC News*, "Indonesia Toll From Tsunami Disaster Rises to 238,946," January 28, 2005, <http://www.bloomberg.com/apps/news?pid=10000080&sid=a40T9tNz2tbM&refer=asia> (February 4, 2005).

8. "Did Island Tribes Use Ancient Lore to Evade Tsunami?" January 25, 2005, <http://news.nationalgeographic.com/news/2005/01/0125_050125_tsunami_island.html> (January 27, 2005).

9. Mark Lallanilla, "Tsunami Epidemics Still a Risk," n.d., <http://abcnews.go.com/Health/Tsunami/story?id=444662&page=1> (February 4, 2005); "U.S. Carrier Ends Disaster Relief Duty," *Houston Chronicle*, February 4, 2005, p. A1.

10. Michael A. Fletcher, "Bush Promises Long-Term U.S. Tsunami Aid," January 11, 2005 <http://www.washingtonpost.com/wp-dyn/articles/A64167-2005Jan10.html> (February 5, 2005); "Clinton Selected As Tsunami Envoy," *Houston Chronicle*, February 2, 2005, p. A1.

11. "Tsunami: Long-term Rural Recovery Needed," January 19, 2005 <http://www.une.eud.au/new/archives/0000147.html> (February 5, 2005).

12. Krishan Francis, "Tsunami Child 'Baby 81,' Parents Reunited," *Associated Press*, Yahoo! News, February 16, 2005, <http://news.yahoo.com/> (February 16, 2005).

13. Ibid.

14. Ibid.

15. Jim Loney, "Asia Quake, Tsunami Moved Islands, Shortened Days," Reuters, *Yahoo! News*, February 10, 2005, <http://news.yahoo.com/> (February 25, 2005).

16. Christopher Bodeen, "Seabed at Tsunami's Center Shows Ruptures," Associated Press, *Yahoo! News*, February 11, 2005, <http://news.yahoo.com/> (February 25, 2005).

17. Loney, "Asia Quake, Tsunami Moved Islands, Shortened Days."

18. McCreery, telephone interview with author, February 4, 2005.

Glossary

bore—Churning water that is moving over the top of water that is moving in the opposite direction.

crest—The top of a wave.

debris—Scattered pieces of something that has been destroyed.

distant tsunami—Giant wave that occurs as the result of an earthquake far away.

earthquake—Shaking of the earth's surface, due to movement of the earth's tectonic plates.

interval—A set time between two actions.

local tsunami—Giant wave that occurs as the result of a nearby earthquake.

mooring lines—Chains or ropes used to tie a ship to a dock.

morgue—A place where dead bodies are stored until burial.

pahoehoe—Hawaiian name for lava that is the hardened shape of flowing molten rock.

peninsula—Land surrounded by water on three sides.

personnel—People who work at a particular workplace or job.

radio direction-finding (DF) station—A radio station that sends out signals to guide ships and airplanes.

run-up wave—The high point reached by a tsunami wave.

seabed—The ocean floor.

seawall—A stone or concrete wall that forms a barrier against the ocean.

seismic—Earth's vibration; something having to do with earthquakes.

span—A section of a bridge.

spawn—To produce or give birth to.

supervisor—The person in charge of a group of workers.

swell—A long wave that moves through the water without breaking or spilling over.

tectonic plates—Sections of the earth's crust that move over molten material deep below the surface.

trough—The empty space in front of the wave crest.

tsunami—Gigantic wave that strikes with deadly force, usually caused by an underwater earthquake.

tsunami warning—An announcement that a tsunami is approaching.

tsunami watch—An announcement that a tsunami may occur.

wind waves—Waves caused by wind blowing on water.

Drohan, Michele Ingber. *Tsunamis: Killer Waves.* New York: Powerkids Press, 1999.

Flaherty, Michael. *Tidal Waves and Flooding.* Brookfield, Conn.: Copper Beech, 1998.

Sorenson, Margo. *Tsunami!: Death Wave.* Logan, Iowa: Perfection Learning Corporation, 1997.

Souza, D. M. *Powerful Waves.* Minneapolis, Minn.: Carolrhoda Books, 1992.

Thompson, Luke. *Tsunamis.* New York: Children's Press, 2000.

Walker, Jane. *Tidal Waves and Flooding.* New York: Gloucester Press, 1992.

Internet Addresses

Pacific Marine Environmental Laboratory
http://www.pmel.noaa.gov/tsunami

Welcome to Tsunami!
http://www.ess.washington.edu/tsunami/index.html

USGS Western Region Coastal and Marine Geology
http://walrus.wr.usgs.gov/tsunami

"Tsunami, the Great Waves"
http://www.nws.noaa.gov/om/brochures/tsunami.htm

How You Can Help

Here is a list of charitable organizations accepting contributions to help relief efforts and dispossessed families in the wake of the Indian Ocean tsunami of December 26, 2004:

UNICEF
<http://www.unicef.org>

The American Red Cross
Disaster Relief Fund
Phone: 1-800-435-7669
<http://www.redcross.org>

Mercy Corps
Dept. W
P.O. Box 2669
Portland, OR 97208

Phone: 1-800-852-2100
<http://www.mercycorps.org>

For other tsunami relief organizations, visit:
<http://www.google.com/tsunami_relief.html>

Index

A

Alaska, 12, 15–18
Africa, 43, 45
Andaman, 45
Appearance of waves, 9,
    23–24, 25
    receding ocean, 21, 29, 42

B

Baby 81, 43, 49–50
Banda Aceh, 43, 44, 51
Burma, 41
Bush, President George H. W.,
    48
Bush, President George W.,
    48, 51
Bush-Clinton Fund, 48–49

C

Chile, 19, 35, 39
Clinton, President Bill, 48–49

D

DART, 36

E

Earthquakes, 11, 13, 14, 41,
    50, 51

F

Five Chinese Brothers, The,
    30–31

H

Hawaii, 8, 9, 19, 25, 26
    Hilo, 8, 26, 28, 33
    Laupahoehoe, 28, 30,
        33–34, 51
Hokusai, (artist), 23

I

India, 45, 46

Indian Ocean, 41, 42, 50, 51
Indonesia, 43

J

Japan, 13, 19, 23, 48

K

Kalutara, 42
Kauai, 9, 10, 21, 25
Kono, Juliet S., (poet), 30, 31
Krakatau, Indonesia, 11–12

M

Maldives, 43
Maui, 10, 25
McCreery, Dr. Charles, 51
Molokai, 9, 10

N

Nicobar, 45
NOAA, 35, 36

P

Pacific Tsunami Museum, 33,
    36
Pacific Tsunami Warning
    Center (PTWC), 34–37,
    41, 51
Papua New Guinea, 13

R

Ring of Fire, 51

S

Safety rules, 21–24, 40
Scotch Cap Lighthouse,
    Alaska, 15–18, 38
Sri Lanka, 43, 50
Sumatra, 41–43, 45, 47, 50
Survivor stories (1946):
    Billena, Carol, 29–30
    Chow, Bob "Steamy", 28, 33

De Caires, Janet, 30, 31
Fujimoto, Bunji, 30
Gusukuma, Yasu, 7–8
Herkes, Jim, 28
Heuer, Kapua, 8
Kanzaki, Frank, 29
Lee, Tuk Wah, 27
Nishimoto, Herbert, 32, 33
Rasmussen, Wayne, 26
Shepherd, Francis, 7
Silva, Martha, 30
Tallett, Paul, 8
Yasuhara, Albert, 27–28
Survivor Stories (2004):
  Jeyarajah, Abilass, 49–50.
    See also Baby 81.
  Jeyarajah, Jenita, 49–50
  Jeyarajah, Murugupillai,
    49–50

T
Thailand, 43
Tsunami Awareness Month,
  33
Tsunami, local/distant, 38
Tsunami, name
  false names, 11
  Japanese origin, 11
Tsunami, 1946, Hawaii
  cost, 19
  damage, 28
  death toll
    Hawaii's worst, 9

individual islands, 18, 21,
  25, 26
most studied, 34
source, 19
total, 33
Tsunami preparedness
  Hawaii Civil Defense, 38
  watch/warning, 36, 38
Tsunami Warning Systems
  International TWS, 35
  Pacific TWS, 34–36
  West Coast and Alaska
    TWS, 38
Tsunami waves
  arrival times, 22–23
  crest/trough, 22–24
  detection, 19–21, 36
  direction, 16, 19
  movement, 24–25
  origin, 11–13
  power, 10, 16, 24–25
  speed, 16, 19, 38
  travel time, 22–23

U
U.S.S. *Brigham Victory*, 26–27
U.S.S. *Lexington*, 47
UNICEF, 49
United Nations, 49–51

W
West Coast, North America,
  39–40

Other titles in the *American Disasters* series:

Apollo 1 Tragedy
Fire in the Capsule
ISBN 0-7660-1787-7

Attack on America
The Day the Twin Towers
Collapsed
ISBN 0-7660-2118-1

Blackout!
Cities in Darkness
ISBN 0-7660-2110-6

The Challenger Disaster
Tragic Space Flight
ISBN 0-7660-1222-0

**Columbine High School
Shooting**
Student Violence
ISBN 0-7660-1782-6

El Niño & La Niña
Deadly Weather
ISBN 0-7660-1551-3

The Exxon Valdez
Tragic Oil Spill
ISBN 0-7660-1058-9

The Hindenburg Disaster
Doomed Airship
ISBN 0-7660-1554-8

Fire in Oakland, California
Billion-Dollar Blaze
ISBN 0-7660-1220-4

Hurricane Andrew
Nature's Rage
ISBN 0-7660-1057-0

Johnstown Flood
The Day the Dam Burst
ISBN 0-7660-2109-2

Jonestown Massacre
Tragic End of a Cult
ISBN 0-7660-1789-2

Love Canal
Toxic Waste Tragedy
ISBN 0-7660-1553-X

Mount St. Helens Volcano
Violent Eruption
ISBN 0-7660-1552-1

**The Oklahoma City
Bombing**
Terror in the Heartland
ISBN 0-7660-1061-9

Pan Am Flight 103
Terrorism Over Lockerbie
ISBN 0-7660-1788-5

Pearl Harbor
Deadly Surprise Attack
ISBN 0-7660-1783-4

Polio Epidemic
Crippling Virus Outbreak
ISBN 0-7660-1555-6

The Siege at Waco
Deadly Inferno
ISBN 0-7660-1218-2

The Titanic
Disaster at Sea
ISBN 0-7660-1557-2

Three Mile Island
Nuclear Disaster
ISBN 0-7660-1556-4

**Triangle Shirtwaist
Factory Fire**
Flames of Labor Reform
ISBN 0-7660-1785-0

Tsunami
Monster Waves
ISBN 0-7660-1786-9

**The World Trade Center
Bombing**
Terror in the Towers
ISBN 0-7660-1056-2

Tsunami